PUSS IN BOOTS, JR. AND THE GOOD GRAY HORSE

INSIGHT PUBLICA®

Nadakkavu, Kozhikode, Kerala, 673011
www.insightpublica.com
e-mail: insightpublica@gmail.com
Title: **PUSS IN BOOTS, JR. AND THE GOOD GRAY HORSE**
Author: **DAVID CORY**
First Insight Edition: May 2025
Printed and Published by
InsightinPublica Printers & Publishers Pvt. Ltd.
ISBN: 978-93-5517-704-9
₹ 190

PUSS IN BOOTS, JR. AND THE GOOD GRAY HORSE

DAVID CORY

INSIGHT PUBLICA

CONTENTS

THE MAGIC WINGS

ONE morning as little Puss, Junior, on his Good Gray Horse rode through Mother Goose country he saw a spider sitting in her tiny lace house. She kept very still, for the early dewdrops still clung to the delicate web. And as the sun shone down they looked for all the world like diamonds on a piece of lace. So little Puss, Junior, stretched out his paw and, would you believe it, instead of a drop of water he picked off a real diamond.

"Ha, ha!" cried the little black spider. "The witch's feather in your hat has changed the dewdrop into a diamond. But I have no use for precious stones, so you may have it. The flies that come to my net are more to my liking." And then she tied the strings of her little black bonnet and put on her black silk mitts and waited for a fly to make a call.

Well, after putting the diamond in his pocket, Puss rode away, and by and by, after a while he came to a steep hill. And, oh, dear me! it was a dreadfully steep hill, for Puss had missed his way and there was no path or road for him to follow. And while he waited, not knowing what to do, he heard a little voice say:

"If I bring four wings to you

To fasten on your horse's shoe

Will you give me for my locket

The sparkling diamond in your pocket?"

"How do I know my Good Gray Horse can fly with these wings?" asked Puss.

"He may try them first," said the voice, and out from behind a stump jumped a little dwarf, dressed in green, with a red turban on his head. Quick as a wink he fastened a wing to each foot of the Good Gray Horse. And then he clicked his tongue against his teeth and away went the Good Gray Horse up in the air like a great bird.

"Hold on!" shouted the dwarf. "Don't forget to give me the diamond," and he held out his little hat for Puss to drop it in as the Good Gray Horse sailed away on his winged feet over the mountain.

Well, as soon as he crossed the top of the great high mountain he came down to earth and, strange to say, as soon as he touched the ground the wings on his feet changed into long, silky hairs, and, but for these, he was just the same as he was before meeting the dwarf.

"Come, little master, since I have lost my wings, to yonder inn. I am hungry for oats." So Puss rode forward and, after leaving him in the stable, sat down in the inn and waited for his dinner. Pretty soon a little bird settled on the window sill and sang:

"From my snug little nest in the old apple tree,

All covered with blossoms so fair,

I never have seen, though I'm over thirteen,

A horse that could fly thro' the air."

Just then the innkeeper's wife came in, and when she saw the little bird on the window sill close to Puss, Junior, she cried, "Time for little birds to be in their nests." So the little

bird flew away, and as soon as Puss had eaten his dinner he again mounted his Good Gray Horse. After a while he met an old man and a little dog. The little dog was carrying a basket in his mouth and the little old man a big pipe, from which the smoke curled up in the shape of a bird. All of a sudden he gave a puff and, would you believe it, a glossy gray pigeon flew away.

Pretty soon the smoke again curled up from the pipe into the form of a pigeon, and then, just as before, the little old man gave a puff, and away flew a pigeon, only this time it was grayish blue.

I don't know how long this would have gone on if the little old man had not suddenly turned around.

"You have a wonderful pipe," said little Puss, Junior. "I've never seen one like it."

"There are lots of strange things in Mother Goose Land," answered the little old man. "If you are a traveler, as I think you are, you will meet with many strange adventures."

Then with a bow he turned in at the gate of a little pink-and-blue cottage, at the rear of which stood a pigeon house on top of a tall pole. As Puss turned around for a last look, again the smoke from the little old man's pipe changed into a pigeon, which flew straight toward the little pigeon house.

Well, after that Puss rode along for some time, and by and by the moon came out and dimly lighted the road, which now led through a forest. It was very quiet, except for the tooting of an owl or the cry of a tree toad.

Little Puss commenced to whistle when, all of a sudden, the Good Gray Horse jumped to the side of the road, and there, right in front of him, stood a tiny fairy, dressed in green. "Halt, Sir Cat!" he cried, waving his silver wand.

THE HOLD-UP

"Oh, who is so merry, so merry, heigh ho!
As the light-hearted fairy, heigh ho, heigh ho!"

As soon as the little fairy I mentioned in the last story finished his song Puss, Junior's, Good Gray Horse stood up on his hind legs, for he wasn't used to these little people of the forest, you see.

"Whoa, my good steed," cried Puss. "Don't you see it's only a little fairy?"

"Only a little fairy!" cried the forest fay. "I would have you understand, Sir Cat, that I have at my command a million subjects. I have but to sound a call upon my silver horn and they will surround you."

"Bah!" cried Puss, scornfully. "I have no fear of such tiny things."

But, oh, dear me! no sooner had he said this than the fairy blew a shrill blast upon his silver horn, and from all directions came thousands of little fairies on moth millers and fireflies. And, oh, dear me! again, before Puss knew what was going to happen they stretched tiny ropes about his Good Gray Horse and bound his legs fast, and after that they tied Puss to the saddle.

"Ha, ha!" laughed the little fairy. "Now, my good Sir Cat, will you believe that fairies have power?"

"Gid-ap!" cried Puss, but his good gray steed could move neither head nor foot. "Gid-ap!" he cried again; but his Good Gray Horse could move neither ears nor tail.

"Gracious me!" exclaimed Puss. "I'm in a pretty mess!" And then the fairies began to sing:

"Pride must ever have a fall.

Ne'er despise the weak and small.

Only he who's brave and good

Shall pass safely through this wood."

"I don't see how that applies to me," cried Puss, stoutly. "I may have been a trifle rude, but I maintain I'm brave and good."

Well, just then, all of a sudden, a big kind-hearted owl flew down from his nest in a tree and cut all the fairy ropes with a big pair of scissors. And then he gave a great hoot, which so frightened the fairies that they flew away, helter skelter, into the depths of the forest.

"You have been very kind to me," said Puss. "How shall I repay you?"

"Forget it," said the owl, taking off his gold-rimmed spectacles and wiping his left eye with a yellow silk handkerchief. "If you would get safely out of this forest,

"Follow the path, the moon is still bright.

Take the first turn—the one to the right.

The Willow Tree Inn you'll find in due course,

Where you'll find shelter for you and your horse."

"Thank you," said Puss. "If your directions are as good as your rhyme I shall have no trouble in finding the place."

WILLOW TREE INN

THE moonlight shone brightly on the sign of the Willow Tree Inn as Puss reached up for the big brass knocker. But he wasn't tall enough, so he stood on an empty flower pot and rapped twice on the door.

"Who's there?" asked the innkeeper, poking his head out of the window.

"Puss in Boots, Junior."

"Very well, Master Boots," said the innkeeper. "Rest on the porch till I put on my boots." And pretty soon the door opened and the sleepy innkeeper appeared with a lighted candle in his hand. "Ah, you have a horse," he said. "Come, I will show you the way to the stable."

"Bad luck," cried the innkeeper, as a gust of wind blew out the candle. "The moon is behind a cloud. 'Tis dark. Can you make your way?"

"Never fear," replied Puss. "A cat can see in the dark."

But, goodness me! just as they reached the barn a bat knocked off Puss, Junior's, hat.

"Bat, bat, come under my hat

And I'll give you a slice of bacon,

And when I bake I'll give you a cake,
If I am not mistaken,"
cried the innkeeper.

Puss knocking at the door

"That sounds mighty good to me," said Puss, Junior. "I've had no supper yet, and it's nearly morning."

"So it is," answered the innkeeper. "Well, we'll give your Good Gray Horse a mess of oats and some hay. After that we'll go back to the inn and cook a slice of bacon."

"And when you bake please give me a cake, or I'll be much disappointed," cried Puss.

"I'd rather give it to you than to that old bat," said the innkeeper, closing the stable door and pushing in the bolt. "Of course, he catches lots of mice, but at the same time I don't like him."

"So you like me better?" said Puss.

"Well, we'll wait and see," said the innkeeper. "In the meantime, come in." And he opened the door and led Puss into the kitchen.

THE ROBBER FAIRIES

"COCKS crow in the morn
To tell us to rise,
And he who lies late
Will never be wise;
"For early to bed
And early to rise
Is the way to be healthy
And wealthy and wise."

"Well, I haven't been to bed at all," said Puss. "I was held up in the forest."

"What!" exclaimed the innkeeper. "I had no idea there were robbers about."

"There were no robbers, my good host," said Puss. "You would hardly believe me if I were to relate what actually happened."

"Tell me," said the innkeeper, "while I fry the bacon."

So Puss explained how the fairies had made him captive, although he feared that the good man would doubt the truth of the story. But, instead, the innkeeper said:

"'Tis not the first time, my good Sir Cat, that I have heard of travelers being held up in yonder woods by the fairies. Indeed, they take a mischievous pleasure in waylaying us mortals after sundown."

"Indeed!" said Puss. "Hereafter I shall take great pains to avoid the forest after dark. I had a narrow escape."

Well, pretty soon the innkeeper placed the food upon the table and he and Puss sat down to eat. But, oh, dear me!

they had hardly commenced when they heard a great commotion in the barnyard. Puss rushed to the door just in time to see his Good Gray Horse gallop out of the stable yard with more than a hundred fairies on his back, who drove sharp little thorns into his sides and blew tiny horns in his ears.

"Whoa!" screamed Puss, rushing out-of-doors. The Good Gray Horse, terrified by the cries of the fairies as well as excited by the stings and blows, paid no attention to the voice of his small master, but dashed out upon the highway, and in a few minutes disappeared down the hill.

"What shall I do?" cried Puss, in dismay.

BICYCLE PUSS

"IF I had a horse in the stable I'd lend him to you," said the kind-hearted innkeeper.

"Have you an automobile?" asked Puss.

"Not yet," replied the innkeeper. "But I have a bicycle which I will lend you."

It took Puss but a moment to mount, and then off he went to catch his Good Gray Horse, who, you remember in the last story, had been stolen by the fairies.

But, oh, dear me! although it was early morning it seemed as if everybody was up and out for a walk. First, an old rooster stood right in the middle of the road and crowed:

"Cock-a-doodle do,

Your horse has lost a shoe."

"Where is it?" asked Puss, stopping as quickly as he could, while the good-natured rooster hopped into the long grass and picked it up.

"Thank you," said Puss, hanging the shoe over his handlebar and setting off once more.

But, oh, dear me! again, he had gone but a short distance when a curly-tailed pig got right in his way, and of course

Puss had to slow up.

"If you're looking for a runaway horse, you'd better take the lane to your right," said the pig, with a grunt and a twist of his curly tail.

So Puss set off again. But, oh, dear me! for the third time, just in front of him was a big, fat cow who had to walk very carefully not to touch the fence rails on either side of her. Puss rang his bell, but she paid no attention to him whatever. She kept right on, swinging her tail from side to side to brush off the flies. And maybe Puss never would have passed her if she hadn't all of a sudden, with a loud moo, trotted into a meadow spread over with butter-cups.

Well, after a little way, Puss almost ran into a big load of hay, and if the farmer had kept on going down the road instead of turning into a gate, I guess Puss would have never caught up with his Good Gray Horse.

"Gracious me!" said Puss, when the road was clear, "I must make up for lost time." But just then a big black crow, who was sitting on a fence post, called out:

"Where are you going so fast, Sir Cat?

Look out, or the wind will blow off your hat."

And he flew off the fence and settled on the handlebar.

"Oh, don't worry! You'll get him, all right," said the crow when Puss told him what a hard time he was having to overtake his Good Gray Horse. "I saw him go by a few minutes ago. He looked pretty tired." And then the old black bird flew away to tell Mrs. Crow that he had seen a pussy cat in boots riding a bicycle.

PUSS RECOVERS HIS STEED

THE girl in the lane, that couldn't speak plain,
Cried, "Gobble, gobble, gobble!"
The man on the hill, that couldn't stand still,
Went hobble, hobble, hobble!

"Goodness me!" exclaimed Puss, Junior, as he mounted the bicycle which the kind owner of the Willow Tree Inn had lent him, "I can't understand a word the girl says. I asked her if she had seen my Good Gray Horse and she answers, 'Gobble, gobble, gobble!'" And then little Puss gave a great sigh, for it's pretty hard luck to have your horse stolen while asleep in a strange inn, although it's mighty lucky to have the innkeeper lend you his bicycle.

Well, after a while and many a mile, the road began to wind up a hill, so Puss got off and pushed his wheel ahead until by and by he met a little old man. He held a stick in both hands, on which he leaned as he hobbled along.

"Did you see a runaway horse?" asked Puss.

"I did, indeed, my good Sir Cat," answered the hobble-hobble man. "He went by but a few minutes ago. There were fairies on his back. I thought at first I must be dreaming, till I remembered once before in my life seeing a swarm of fairies, if I might use the word, from yonder forest in hot pursuit for a bold robber who had waylaid a traveler."

The Hobble-Hobble Man

"Thank you," said Puss. "I must catch up with them, for the horse belongs to me, and this bicycle is a poor substitute."

"Yes, I should think as much," replied the hobble-hobble man. "But how are you going to catch him? Those forest fairies are mischievous, and you will need to pedal fast and

furious to overtake them."

"Never fear," replied Puss, stoutly. "I have a good pair of legs." And, jumping on his bicycle, he went up the hill at a great rate. On reaching the top he was delighted to see his Good Gray Horse going down the road to the valley.

"Here's where I overtake them," cried Puss, placing his feet on the coasters. "My bicycle can go downhill faster than a horse. In a few moments I'll again be astride my faithful steed."

The dust flew out in a cloud behind him as he swiftly coasted down the steep road. Ting-a-ling, ting-a-ling! went his bell as he came nearer and nearer. "Gid-ap!" cried the fairies, but the Good Gray Horse was tired. He had gone many miles at a gallop.

"Whoa!" cried Puss.

"Gid-ap!" cried the fairies.

But Puss was now close to them. Standing up on the bicycle seat, he made a wonderful jump and landed squarely on the saddle of his Good Gray Horse. And then, with a scream of dismay, the fairies flew away.

GEORGY PORGY

NOW let me see. In the last story Puss had taken his Good Gray Horse away from the fairies, but didn't know what to do with the bicycle which he had borrowed from the owner of the Willow Tree Inn! "I can't very well ride it and lead my horse," said Puss to himself, "nor can I very well ride my horse and lead the bicycle. What shall I do?"

A short distance off stood a small red schoolhouse and just then through the open door came a merry crowd of children. All of a sudden a little boy with a piece of plum pudding in one hand and a piece of pie in the other ran swiftly toward Puss.

Georgy Porgy, pudding and pie,
Kissed the girls and made them cry.
When the boys came out to play
Georgy Porgy ran away

And after him came a number of boys in hot pursuit. "Please help me get away from these boys!" cried Georgy Porgy.

"What have you done?" asked Puss.

"Oh, I kissed the girls and made them cry," answered

Georgy Porgy, "but it didn't hurt them."

"How do you know?" asked Puss.

"Kisses don't hurt," replied Georgy Porgy.

"But if these boys ever catch me"—looking fearfully over his shoulder—"they'll give me an awful beating and take away my pie."

"Do you know where the Willow Tree Inn is?" asked Puss, all of a sudden.

"Yes, siree—," answered Georgy.

"Quick!" cried Puss. "Get on this bicycle and take it to the innkeeper. He lent it to me."

But, oh, dear me! the boys were now close at hand and Georgy Porgy had only time enough to give Puss the pie and pudding. "Take 'em," he said, "I sha'n't have time to eat 'em. I can't eat and ride at the same time!"

"Go it!" shouted Puss, and, goodness me! how that bicycle did go!

"Stop! Stop!" yelled the boys.

"Go it!" screamed Puss. "Don't let them catch you!"

And Georgy Porgy didn't! No, siree! Then all of a sudden the recess bell rang, and of course the boys had to turn back.

"I think I'll be jogging along, too," said Puss to himself. "They might throw a stone at me for helping Georgy." And he galloped past the schoolhouse and was soon out of sight.

A JOLLY GALLOP

"WELL, well, well!" cried Puss, Junior, to himself, as he pulled in his Good Gray Horse after leaving the little red schoolhouse far behind. "It was lucky for me that Georgy Porgy happened to come my way. Otherwise, how would I have been able to return the bicycle to the innkeeper?" And after that he walked his horse until he came to a stream, on the banks of which stood an old mill. The mill pond was rimmed with overhanging willow trees, and the water trickled over the dam with a soft, gurgling noise. Through the sluiceway the water ran in a swift stream, turning the old wheel around and around.

Puss dismounted, and after his horse had taken a drink he cropped the fresh green grass, while Puss lay down in the shade.

"Margaret wrote a letter,
Sealed it with her finger,
Threw it in the dam
For the dusty miller.
Dusty was his coat,
Dusty was the siller,
Dusty was the kiss

From the dusty miller.
If I had my pockets
Full of gold and siller,
I would give it all
To my dusty miller."

Goodness me! Puss must have fallen asleep in the shade of the old willow tree. It was a sleepy place, and the water trickling over the dam made one dream of silver fishes! Puss rubbed his eyes and listened:

"If I had my pockets

Full of gold and siller,

I would give it all

To my dusty miller."

"Would you really?" asked Puss, looking up at a pretty girl leaning against a tree close by. It was she who had sung this little song, you see.

"Oh, dear me! I thought I was all alone," she sighed.

"So did I," said Puss, "until you woke me."

"Were you asleep?" asked the pretty girl.

"Asleep and dreaming," answered our small hero.

"So was I—I mean I was dreaming," said the pretty girl, in a low voice.

"Yonder stands my Good Gray Horse. Would you like to ride with me?" asked Puss.

"Yes, indeed," replied the girl, quickly. "Take me for a jolly gallop." And the next minute she and Puss, Junior, were racing down the road.

THE RUNAWAY

"MERRY are the bells, and merry would they ring;
Merry was myself, and merry could I sing;
With a merry ding-dong, happy, gay, and free,
And a merry sing-song, happy let us be.
"Merry have we met, and merry have we been,
Merry let us part, and merry meet again;
With our merry sing-song, happy, gay, and free,
And a merry ding-dong, happy let us be."

"Whoa!" cried Puss, Junior, pulling in his Good Gray Horse.

"You've given me a lovely ride," said the pretty girl. "It is more than a mile from the mill. I live just over there," pointing to a cottage on the hillside.

"Shall I take you up to the gate?" asked Puss. "No, I'll get off here, thank you," she replied, "and I shall never forget how nice you've been. I was quite unhappy before you spoke to me at the old mill pond."

"Merry have we met, and merry have we been,
Merry let us part, and merry meet again,"
said Puss, stretching out his paw.

"How well you remember my song!" said the pretty girl, waving her hand to Puss as he rode away.

Horse and wagon

He had gone but a short distance when he heard the clatter of hoofs. Looking back, he was startled to see a horse and wagon come tearing down the road.

"A runaway!" he exclaimed, quickly drawing to one side. In a few minutes the frightened horse rushed by. In the wagon was a little old man, clinging tightly to the reins and with great difficulty keeping his horse in the middle of the road. In an instant Puss set off in pursuit. Pretty soon his Good Gray Horse drew close to the wagon. "Don't give up!" cried Puss. "Hold on tight!" The little old man did his best, but by this time his horse had become unmanageable and, turning suddenly to the right, dashed up a steep bank. With a snap, the harness broke and away went the frightened animal.

"Let the pesky brute go," exclaimed the old man. "He'll get tired of running and come home by and by."

"You may have my horse," cried Puss. And in a few minutes the harness was mended and Puss and the little old man drove off down the road.

HUMPTY-BUMPTY

HUMPTY-BUMPTY, bump! went the wagon, as the Good Gray Horse trotted along. "Very poor springs on this wagon," cried Puss, his teeth knocking together as they crossed a rough bit of road.

"You are not used to farm wagons, my good Sir Cat," the little old man replied.

"You are right," said Puss.

"Did you ever hear the conundrum in rhyme about

"'Thirty white horses upon a red hill,

Now they tramp, now they champ,

Now they all stand still'?"

asked the little old man.

"No," replied Puss. "But who ever saw a red hill?"

"Ha, ha!" laughed the little old man, showing how very few teeth he had to chatter. "Why, the thirty white horses are your teeth, and the red hill is your gums. Ha, ha!"

"He, he!" laughed Puss. "Gid-ap, my Good Gray Horse. Let us rattle the thirty white horses upon a red hill, let them tramp and champ, but never stand still!" And away went the wagon clattering after the Gray Horse, bumpty-bumpty, bump!

"Hold on!" cried the little old man. "If I have but few teeth, I have old bones! Do you wish to shake me to bits?"

"Whoa!" cried Puss, but the Good Gray Horse evidently thought it great fun, for on he went at a still faster clip. The boards in the bottom of the wagon flew up and down and the wooden seat swayed back and forth. Up and down, bumpty-bumpty, bump! went the little old man.

"Pull him in!" he cried. "Pull on the lines! Don't let your horse run away!"

Puss tugged at the reins, but the Good Gray Horse had the bit between his teeth. He stuck out his head and tail and let his feet fly. Over the stones bumped the wagon, up on one side and then down on the other. Poor Puss had all he could do to keep from falling out, and the little old man clung to the side boards and cried, "Pull on the lines!"

"I am," panted Puss, "but it doesn't do any good."

"Pull harder!" yelled the little old man.

"Can't," replied Puss, now breathless from the bumping of the wagon. "Can't pull one little bit harder."

"Turn him in yonder lane!" screamed the little old man. "That's my lane! It leads into the barnyard."

Well, it was mighty lucky that Puss managed to turn up the lane, and in another moment they were racing into the yard, but before Puss could stop him the Good Gray Horse went head first into the haymow and headlong over the dashboard went Puss and the little old man.

THE HAYMOW

IT was a mighty lucky thing that the Good Gray Horse in the last story ran into the haymow instead of the corn-crib. Well, as soon as Puss picked himself up the Good Gray Horse pulled his head out of the haymow. He had gone in quite deep, for he was going at a great rate, and it's a wonder he didn't go right through the great mound of hay.

"Whew! Miew!" cried Puss, pulling wisps of hay out of his hair and dusting off the tops of his red boots. "That was a pretty sudden stop!"

"Yes, but it turned out all right," said the little old man. "It was about the best way to stop your horse, methinks. It was lucky there was hay in the way, I should say."

"How could you be such a bad old thing?" asked Puss, stroking the Good Gray Horse on the nose. "The idea of your running away with us!"

The Good Gray Horse made no reply, however. He looked a little foolish, but, beyond that, he seemed very much the same, except that his collar was pushed up over his ears and his harness twisted about his neck.

"Well, put him in the stable," said the little old man. "We'll give him a good bed and some oats. My own horse may show up some time this evening—that is, if he ever gets tired of running."

Into the Hay Mow

After the Good Gray Horse was made comfortable the little old man led Puss, Junior, into the house.

"Mother," he called out, as he opened the door, "here is a visitor for you."

A queer little old woman arose from her rocking chair and came forward. "What! a cat!" she exclaimed, throwing up her hands in dismay. "John, you know I don't like cats!"

"Then, madam," said Puss, Junior, politely, "I'll not trespass on your hospitality," and he turned to leave.

"Not so, not so!" cried the little old man. "Mother, you don't understand what has happened. This noble cat has done me a good turn. My old mare ran away and he kindly hitched up his Good Gray Horse to my wagon and brought me home."

"Ah," said the little old man's wife, "that's another story. This cat is no ordinary cat. Let him make himself comfortable while I go and see about supper."

But Puss still hesitated.

"You are indeed welcome," said the little old woman, peering over her glasses to get a good look at him; "you shall stay and rest yourself, for you have helped my good man, and whoever does my man a good turn shall never go unrewarded."

CHAUFFEUR TAFFY

"HIGH-HO, how the winds blow!" exclaimed little Puss, Junior, as he rode along on his Good Gray Horse toward the castle of my Lord Carabas to see his dear father, Puss in Boots.

But New Mother Goose Land is a big country and Puss did not realize how long a journey it was. You see, he had been seeking adventures for so long and had traveled so far—sometimes on the back of his good friend, Goosey Goosey Gander, sometimes in the airship whose captain was a downy goose and the sailors four and twenty doves, and then, again, on broomsticks and umbrellas and baskets that flew in the air with their old women owners—that now, once more astride of his Good Gray Horse who had carried him many a mile in Old Mother Goose Land he felt he would soon be with his father.

Well, as Puss rode along he came to a bend in the road where an automobile stood. It had evidently broken down, for the chauffeur was tinkering with the machinery.

All of a sudden a blackbird perched herself on the fence along the road and began to sing:

"Taffy was a chauffeur, Taffy was a loafer,

Taffy broke a tire everywhere he went.
His master soon grew tired, Taffy he was fired;
Taffy he was fired without another cent.
"Taffy came to master's house; master wasn't in.
Taffy made an awful row, kicked up such a din.
He blew on his auto horn, blew with all his might;
Everyone but Taffy ran away in fright."

"Whoa there!" cried Puss, Junior, and the blackbird must have thought it was meant for her, for she stopped her song and looked at our small hero. And of course the Good Gray Horse stopped, and Taffy—well, he crawled out from under the automobile and scowled at the blackbird. And this made Puss, Junior, laugh, and the Good Gray Horse cough and the blackbird snicker, all of which made Taffy very red in the face.

"Tell-tale-tit, your tongue shall be slit," he cried, but the blackbird clapped her wings and flew away. And after that Puss, Junior, said gid-ap to his horse and rode off, leaving Taffy to finish mending his automobile. And after a little while the blackbird came back and settled herself on the head of the Good Gray Horse.

"Where are you going?" she said.

"To visit my father, Puss in Boots," replied our little hero.

THREE LITTLE KITTENS

THREE little kittens lost their mittens
And they began to cry,
"Oh, mother dear, we very much fear
That we have lost our mittens."

"I'll help you find them," cried Puss, Junior, looking in through the door of a little green house.

"Will you?" said a little tabby cat.

"I think we lost them by the woodpile," said a little gray kitten.

"Perhaps we dropped them while playing hide and go seek," said a cute black kitty.

"Come on, my little pussyfoots," cried Puss, Junior, with a grin. "I'm pretty good at finding things—except people—I can't find my dear father."

"How did you lose him?" asked the first little kitty, as they all ran out into the back yard.

"I don't know any more than you know how you lost your mittens," replied Puss, Junior, with a laugh.

"If you find our mittens we'll help you find your father," cried the three little kittens. But, hunt as they might, no mittens were to be found. Under the woodpile and back of the old well, behind the woodshed and under the grape arbor, they hunted, but in vain.

Puss and Mittens

"You naughty kittens! Lost your mittens! Then you shall have no pie!"

"Mee-ow, mee-ow, mee-ow."

"No, you shall have no pie."

"Mee-ow, mee-ow, mee-ow."

"Have you looked in the barn?" asked Puss.

"No," cried the three little kittens.

"Well, that's a good place to look if you've been playing there," suggested Puss. So they all ran out to the barn. But just as they entered the big door a little mouse scurried into a hole and a big gray rat ran into the corn bin.

"Look here, little mouse, if you'll tell us whether you've seen any mittens we won't hurt you," cried Puss. But the little mouse didn't reply.

"My dear Mr. Rat," said Puss, Junior, speaking into a crack of the corn bin, "if you'll tell us whether you have seen any mittens we'll promise not to touch you." But the rat didn't answer.

"They're afraid of you," said the little black kitty.

"Then you ask them," whispered Puss, Junior.

"Did you see our mittens?" whispered the black kitty to the little mouse.

"Yes," replied a squeaky voice. "I saw some mittens in the tool closet." Then the little black kitty ran over to the tool closet, and pretty soon he came dancing out on his two hind legs. "Here they are! Here they are!" he cried, with a happy purr.

MR. RAT

THE three little kittens found their mittens,
And they began to cry,
"Oh, mother dear, see here, see here!
See, we have found our mittens."

"Thank you," said the black kitty, as the little mouse peeped out of her house, "thank you very much for telling us where our mittens were."

"We promise never to hurt you," cried the three little kittens.

Puss, Junior, walked over to the corn bin. "Look here, Mr. Rat," he said, in a gruff voice, "as long as you were so mean not to tell us where the mittens were, I won't promise not to catch you."

"You'd better wait till you get the chance," replied the rat, looking down from the top of the bin.

"Just wait till we grow up, Mr. Rat," said the three little kittens, looking very fierce with their whiskers standing out straight from their little fat cheeks and their tails twice their natural size. "You had better not be too sure of yourself.

"For many a rat who has spoken like that
Has been caught when he least was aware.
So you'd better look out what you are about,

For we are three kittens who dare."

"That's the way to talk to him," said Puss, Junior, admiringly. "We'll scare him to death, anyway."

"No, you won't," said the rat. "You don't know who I am. I'm the rat 'that ate the malt that lay in the house that Jack built.'"

"Oh, you are, are you?" said Puss. "Well, what are you doing here?"

"Making a visit," replied the rat.

"Look out," advised Puss, "or you may not find it a pleasant one."

"Nonsense!" replied the rat with a loud laugh. "Who's afraid of three little kittens? They can't even find their mittens." Before he had time to say another word Puss, Junior, sprang on top of the corn bin. Away went the rat, over the barn floor, out through the open door, down the path to the road. Puss, Junior, kicked off his red-topped boots and went after him.

"Go it, Puss, dear!" screamed three little kittens. "Catch him!"

The ground was covered with a light fall of snow, but this made no difference to Puss, Junior. He was a big, strong, healthy cat, and he didn't mind running barefoot in the snow. This was not the case with Mr. Rat, however. Very soon his feet became so cold that he could hardly run, and before he reached the gate Puss pounced upon him.

"Look here," said Puss, fiercely, holding him down on the frozen ground—"look here, Mr. Rat, we don't want you around here any longer. Do you understand?"

"I'll promise to go back to Jack's house if you'll let me up."

"All right," said Puss. "Now go!" And away went the frightened rat.

A BIG TUMBLE

"PUT on your mittens, you silly kittens,
And you shall have some pie.
Purr-r, purr-r, purr-r."
"Oh, let us have the pie,
Purr-r, purr-r, purr-r."

Mrs. Cat stood in the doorway of her little house and again she called out, "Put on your mittens, you silly kittens."

"And I'll pull on my boots," said Puss, Junior, running back to the barn. "My toes are almost frozen."

"Has the horrid old rat really gone?" asked the three little kittens.

"He has," replied Puss. "Didn't you see me catch him just before he reached the gate?"

"There was so much snow flying about that we couldn't see very well," said the gray kitten.

"Well, I caught him, all right," replied Puss, pulling on his boots, "but he begged me so hard to let him go that I did. He promised he'd never come back."

"If he really is the 'rat that ate the malt that lay in the house that Jack built' I don't believe Jack will be very glad to see him," said the little tabby cat, pulling on her mittens.

"My paws are almost frozen," cried the little gray kitten. "I'm so glad we have found our mittens."

"Good-by, mousie," cried the little black kitten, going up to the mouse hole and peeping in. "We all thank you very much for telling us where our mittens were. We're going into the house now, for mother has some pie for us. We'll bring you out a little piece of crust in a few minutes."

"Don't forget!" she answered, peeping out of her hole. "Bring us three pieces, for I have two little children who are very fond of pie crust."

"You be sure to save a little piece of crust," said the black kitty to the tabby kit, "and you, too," he said, turning to the gray kitten; "then we'll have three pieces!"

"Let's close the barn door," said Puss, before they started off for the house. "The little mouse may freeze if we leave it open."

It was a very big barn door that ran on little iron wheels, and it wasn't easy to move. "Push!" cried Puss, bracing his feet against the side of the barn.

"We can't push any harder," cried the three little kittens.

"Try again," said Puss. "Now, all together, heave ho, heave ho!" The big door began to move. "Push!" cried Puss. "It's beginning to move."

The three little kittens did their best, and pretty soon the little wheels went round and round, faster and faster, until all of a sudden the big door bumped into the other end of the doorway, sending Puss, Junior, and the three little kittens head over heels into the snow.

HUNGRY KITTENS

"GOODNESS, what a bump!" cried the little black kitty, wiping the snow from his eyes.

"Gracious! what a bump!" said Puss, scrambling up from the ground. "I think I felt it more than the old barn door, for I was underneath, you see, and you were piled on top of me."

The three little kittens felt very sorry and commenced to brush the snowflakes from his fur coat. "There's snow in your boot legs," said the little gray kitten, standing on tiptoe and looking down Puss, Junior's, boots. "Don't you feel it? I should think it would make you shiver."

"I'll soon find out," said Puss, pulling them off and turning them upside down.

"Are they wet inside?" asked the tabby kitten, anxiously.

"Not very," said Puss, squinting up one eye and peering in.

"If they are," said the little black kitten, "mother will dry them for you at the fire."

Then:

The three little kittens put on their mittens,

And soon ate up the pie.

"Oh, mother dear, we greatly fear

That we have soiled our mittens."

While Puss was busy placing his boots before the kitchen stove the three little kittens seated themselves at the table.

Puss shaking out his boot

"Why don't you take off your mittens?" Puss asked. "I guess you're so hungry you can't wait," he added with a laugh.

It took but a short time for his boots to dry, for there was a big, blazing fire in the stove.

"Don't you want something to eat?" asked Mrs. Cat, coming over to Puss. "You have very pretty boots," she continued, lifting up one and looking at it with much admiration.

"Yes, they are nice boots," said Puss, Junior. "They were made for my famous father, Puss in Boots. Mr. Solomon Grundy, who was born on a Monday, made them years ago for my father. And one day, it was only last week, when I stopped at his store, I saw a notice in his window that he had died on Saturday and was buried on Sunday, and that was the end of Solomon Grundy."

"Too bad," said Mrs. Cat.

"When I went into the store," continued Puss, "Mrs. Grundy took them down from a shelf and sold them to me. Then she went across the street to ask an old friend where my father lived, but she couldn't find out—her friend didn't know or couldn't remember—so here I am, still searching for my daddy."

"Too bad," said Mrs. Cat again. "I'm really very sorry. But do not give up hope, for you will find him I am sure."

KITTENS WASH MITTENS

AFTER Mrs. Cat had powdered Puss, Junior's, toes so that they would slip easily into his boots she turned to see what the three little kittens were doing. They had just finished eating the pie. She had been so interested in hearing how Puss, Junior, had found his red-top boots that she hadn't heard them say:

"Oh, mother dear, we greatly fear

That we have soiled our mittens."

"What!" exclaimed Mrs. Cat. "Soiled your mittens, you naughty kittens!"

Then they began to sigh,

"Mi-ow, mi-ow, mi-ow."

Then they began to sigh,

"Mi-ow, mi-ow, mi-ow."

"Take them off at once," cried Mrs. Cat.

"We will, mother," said the three little kittens.

"I can't imagine why you kept them on," said Mrs. Cat.

"We were so hungry we didn't have time to take them off," said the little black kitten.

"My fingers were so cold I thought I'd leave them on,"

cried the tabby kitten.

"I didn't think about anything," sobbed the little gray kitten. "I just looked at the pie, and then I forgot I had on mittens."

Mrs. Cat

Mrs. Cat stood with her front paws on her hips, looking first from one little kitten to another.

"Did you ever see anything like children?" she sighed, turning to Puss, Junior.

"My dear madam, forgive them this once. They were so excited over finding the pie that they lost their heads."

"It's a good thing they are tied on," said Mrs. Cat, with a laugh; "they might not be found as easily as the mittens."

The three little kittens looked very much ashamed. Then the little black kitten ran over to the washtubs and, jumping on a stool, turned the hot-water faucet. His mother handed him a big cake of soap, and in another minute the other two little kittens climbed up beside him.

"What are you going to do?" asked Mrs. Cat, with a sly wink at Puss, Junior.

"Never mind, mother, dear. Please don't look." And they commenced to scrub their mittens. And when they had them all covered with lather they dipped them into the water and squeezed them until the soapsuds looked like a snow drift, and after that they all reached down and pulled out the stopper, and when the soapy water was all gone they filled the tub again with nice, clean water and washed the mittens all over again. But, oh, dear me! the water was so deep that the little gray kitten wet her little pink sleeve.

PIE FOR MRS. MOUSE

THE three little kittens washed their mittens
And hung them up to dry.
"Oh, mother dear, do you not hear
That we have washed our mittens?"

Sure enough, all the mittens were washed and neatly hung on the clothesline. But the clothesline was so high that Puss had been forced to climb a stepladder. The kittens had stood below, their little paws full of clothespins, and every time Puss needed a pin one of them had climbed up and handed it to him.

"Washed your mittens! Oh, you're good kittens.
But I smell a rat close by.
Hush! Hush! mee-ow, mee-ow.
We smell a rat close by,
Mee-ow, mee-ow, mee-ow!"
cried Mrs. Cat.

When Puss heard this he ran around the house. I guess he expected to find the "rat that ate the malt that lay in the house that Jack built." But Mrs. Cat had made a mistake, for there was no rat to be seen. Instead, there stood the little mouse who two or three stories ago had told the black kitty where to find their mittens.

"What do you want?" asked Puss, Junior, kindly.

"I think the three little kittens have forgotten their promise to give me three pieces of pie. I've been waiting in the barn all this time."

"Kittens!" cried Puss.

The three little kittens came tumbling around the house. But the little mouse ran behind a tree.

"Did you forget to save some pie crust for the little mouse and her two children?" asked Puss.

"Of course not!" replied the three kittens.

"I tucked a little piece under my plate," said the gray kitten.

"I put a little piece in the old clock," said the tabby kitten.

"And I put mine behind the big shell on the mantelpiece," cried the black kitty.

"Go and get them," said Puss, "for Mrs. Mouse can't be kept waiting; her babies out in the barn will be crying for her."

The three little kittens ran into the house, and pretty soon returned with the pie crust.

"We'll carry it out to the barn for you," they cried.

So the little mouse ran ahead, and when she was safe in the barn she waited until the kittens had placed the three little pieces of pie crust on the floor. As soon as they had gone the little mouse came out and carried the pie crust into her house.

SING A SONG OF SIXPENCE

SING a song of sixpence,
A pocketful of rye,
Four and twenty blackbirds
Baked in a pie.
When the pie was opened
The birds began to sing.
Wasn't that a dainty dish
To set before the king?

Well, when little Puss, Junior, heard those blackbirds singing he halted before the castle and knocked on the gate.

"You must have a thousand canaries."

"Canaries nothing," replied the old retainer. "The King's twenty-four blackbirds are singing."

But, goodness, gracious me! all of a sudden something happened. And it was even worse than when the raven cried, "Croak!" and the farmer's mare fell down and broke her knee. For just then, while

The maid was in the garden
Hanging out the clothes,

Down came a blackbird
And snapped off her nose.

Pretty maid

Perhaps he was angry because he hadn't been invited to sing for the King. I'm sure I don't know, but, anyway, he was a mighty mean bird, let me tell you.

"Oh, dear! Oh, dear!" cried the poor maid, and she sat down on a garden bench and began to weep. Just then the four and twenty blackbirds jumped out of the pie and flew into the garden to look for that naughty bird. But they couldn't find him. Oh, dear, no! He was far away by that time, maybe at the North Pole of Mother Goose Land, which they tell me is a frosted stick of sugar candy.

"Oh, what shall I do?" sobbed the maid, still holding her poor nose in her hands.

"You had better call in the doctor," suggested Puss.

"He lives a good two miles from here," said the old retainer, "and our telephone is out of order."

"I'll go fetch him," said Puss. "Dry your eyes, pretty maid!" And, jumping on his Good Gray Horse, he galloped away. And the four and twenty blackbirds flew after him so that in case the naughty blackbird came back to nip little Puss, Junior's, nose they would be there to protect him.

DOCTOR FOSTER

DOCTOR FOSTER went to Glo'ster

In a shower of rain;

He stepped in a puddle up to his middle,

And never went there again.

Which was a mighty lucky thing, for, goodness knows, perhaps the poor maid never would have had her nose mended if Puss hadn't found the good doctor at home.

Well, as soon as he learned what was the matter, he jumped up behind Puss, and the Good Gray Horse kicked out his heels and galloped away, and the four and twenty blackbirds trailed after them, and pretty soon, not so very long, they came to the Blackbird-pie Castle. There sat the poor maid in the garden, still holding her nose in her hand.

"Let's see it," said the doctor, opening his little black bag and taking out medicine and bandages.

"I'm afraid it's half gone," sobbed the maid, "I don't want to look at it."

Dr. Foster binding up the Maid's nose

"But I do," said the doctor. "Otherwise, how can I mend it?" And I guess he was right, for he was the most famous doctor in all Mother Goose Land. Well, as soon as she took away her hand he said:

"It's not as bad as it might be. It still looks like a nose!"

"Does it?" she sobbed.

"Oh yes," said the doctor, turning to Puss and the old retainer. "You'll hardly know the blackbird touched it after I get through."

"Maybe he only pinched it," said Puss.

"Or only tweaked it," said the old retainer.

"Perhaps he thought it was a cherry," laughed the doctor, putting on some powder.

And then the maid began to smile. "It feels much better already," she said.

"Well it's always a good thing to call in the doctor," said the learned man. "You never can tell what may happen," and, picking up his little black bag, he held out his hand. "Two shillings, please!"

"Mercy me!" she cried. "I haven't had my wages for this month."

"What did you do with last month's?" asked the doctor, but before she could reply one of the four and twenty blackbirds dropped a gold piece in his hand. I guess he felt dreadfully ashamed to think that one of his brothers had pinched a pretty girl's nose.

A MISCOUNT

THE King was in his counting-house,
Counting out his money;
The Queen was in the parlor,
Eating bread and honey.

And now let us see where little Puss, Junior, was. Oh yes, I remember now. He was in the garden of the Blackbird-pie Castle, where the poor maid's nose had been nipped by a naughty, bad blackbird. Well, after the good Doctor had gone, the old retainer took Puss to see the King, who was so busy counting his money that he didn't even look up.

"Your Worship," began the retainer.

"What do you want?" asked the King, angrily. "I've just counted up to three trillion two hundred and thirty-seven billion, nine hundred and forty-eight million, seven hundred and fifteen thousand, four hundred and—and—now you've gone and made me miss, and I'll have to count all over again."

"Start off at four hundred. A few sovereigns less won't matter to a king," said little Puss, Junior.

"I'm not so sure about that," replied His Majesty, taking off his crown and scratching his head. "One likes to be right as well as King!"

"Nobody said, my lord!" cried the old retainer. "But consider your health. Let's take this wise cat's suggestion and quit for the time being."

"All right," said the King. "Let's go find the Queen."

She was in the parlor eating bread and honey. "How do you do, my dear Puss, Junior?" she cried.

"I am very well, thank Your Majesty," he replied.

"I have just heard what valuable assistance you have rendered our court," continued the Queen.

Puss would have blushed had not his cheeks been covered with whiskers.

"I did but do my duty, Your Majesty," he replied.

"What's that?" asked the King.

"Did you not hear, my lord?" cried the Queen. "Our maid had her nose bitten by a naughty blackbird, and our little friend here quickly fetched the Doctor, bringing him on his Good Gray Horse in short time."

"Indeed!" exclaimed His Majesty. "I will reward him. He shall have a castle and a retinue."

"Your Royal Highness," exclaimed Puss, Junior, "I am overwhelmed with your generosity, but I needs must decline your offer. For until I find my father, the famous Puss in Boots, I may not rest upon my journey except for sleep and refreshment."

Puss kissing the Queen's hand

"Zounds!" exclaimed the King. "You are a gallant cat. Would that all my subjects were as faithful to their duty as you are! But," he added, with a smile, "you shall rest here for the night, for a good dinner and a sound sleep will make you travel the faster on the morrow."

The Queen by this time had finished her bread and honey.

"Come out on the terrace," she suggested, "for it is cool and pleasant there, and the flowers are very beautiful. I would show Sir Cat our flower garden."

The King, therefore, gave his arm to the Queen and Puss gallantly held up her train, the three walking slowly out upon the broad terrace. The sun was quite low in the sky, for it was late in the afternoon. The big hills to the westward seemed to hold up the sky, and Puss wondered whether the jolly old sun would not bump himself as he slid down over the edge of the world.

"Come, Puss dear, take my hand," said the Queen. She then went over and sat down on a marble bench. Picking up Puss, she held him in her arms and commenced to sing, and presently he fell fast asleep. The Queen looked up at the King and said, "Is he not a dear little cat?" and the King for answer took from his purse several gold pieces and tucked them away in Puss, Junior's, pocket.

PLUM PUDDING STORY

WHEN Puss, Junior, awoke from his nap he was surprised to find himself in the Queen's lap. It was growing dark and for a moment he wondered where he was. "Don't ask where you are, my dear Puss," laughed the Queen, "for you are safe and well."

"Your Majesty," said Puss, rubbing his eyes, "I was also very comfortable. Pardon me for dropping off to sleep in your presence."

Just then a page appeared and announced that dinner was served. The King arose and offered his arm to the Queen, Puss following quietly after. As he stepped down the great stairway to the royal dining room he heard some one singing in a deep voice:

"When good King Arthur ruled this land,

He was a goodly King;

He stole three pecks of barley meal

To make a bag pudding.

"A bag pudding the King did make

And stuffed it well with plums,

And in it put great lumps of fat

As big as my two thumbs.

"The King and Queen did eat thereof,

And noblemen beside;

And what they could not eat that night

The Queen next morning fried."

"Plum pudding!" said Puss to himself. "That sounds pretty nice," and he followed the King and Queen into the great dining hall. Many noblemen were present and the table was a most gorgeous affair. Silver tankards and wonderful gold dishes gleamed in the candlelight. Puss was very much impressed and behaved beautifully. And when the plum pudding came on the table the same deep voice began to sing:

"And what they could not eat that night

The Queen next morning fried."

"Puss," said the Queen in a whisper, "let's finish the pudding between us! I know you'd like some more, and so would I. Moreover," she added in a still lower whisper, "I don't intend getting up early to-morrow morning to fry what's left over—so let us finish it to-night."

Presently the court fool came running in, his fool's cap all ajingle with bells. He capered about, swinging up and down a little stick which was also covered with tiny bells. These were silver, and the ones in his cap were of gold, so that the sound was very sweet.

The next morning Puss mounted his Good Gray Horse and rode away, and after a while he came to a great mound of earth in which was a little wooden door on leather hinges.

"What sort of a house is this?" thought Puss. And then, as if in answer to his question, the door opened and there stood a big brown bear dressed in a fur overcoat. And, oh, dear me! at first Puss was startled, and the Good Gray Horse reared on his hind legs. But the big brown bear didn't growl.

Not even a little bit. He just smiled as only a brown bear can, and said:

"If you have money

I'll sell you some honey."

So Puss jumped down and followed the bear into his hill house, for Puss was curious to see what kind of a home this big, smiling brown bear had, you see.

Well, I want you to know it was a mighty nice sort of a place. There was a big fireplace with great immense crackling logs, and over it, on the mantelpiece, were two beautiful carved candlesticks made from deers' horns, and a cuckoo clock. And just then out came the little cuckoo herself and began to sing.

"ONE I LOVE, TWO I LOVE"

ONE, I love; two, I love;
Three, I love, I say;
Four, I love with all my heart;
Five, I cast away.
Six, he loves; seven, she loves;
Eight, both love.
Nine, he comes; ten, he tarries;
Eleven, he courts, and twelve, he marries.

On a big stone by the wayside sat a little boy and girl. She held a daisy in her hand, from which she slowly picked off the petals as she counted:

"One, I love; two I love."

"Whoa!" cried Puss, Junior.

"Three, I love, I say."

Both the children looked up. "What a dandy cat," cried the little girl, "and what a beautiful horse."

"Give us a ride?" asked the little boy.

"Do you know how to ride?" asked Puss, with a grin.

"I can ride my rocking horse ever so fast," the little boy replied.

"So can I," said the little girl.

"Stand on the stone," said Puss. "I'll ride up close, and then you both can climb up behind me. Easy there!" cried Puss, guiding the Good Gray Horse up to the children, who stood close together on the big high stone. "Now climb up behind me," and in a minute the two children had scrambled on to the saddle. "Gid-ap!" and off went the Good Gray Horse on a canter.

"Isn't this great?" cried the little boy.

"Isn't it lovely?" said the little girl.

"One, I love; two, I love; three, I love, I say; four, I love with all my heart," sang Puss. "There are just four of us. You two and my Good Gray Horse and I."

"But that isn't the way," said the little girl. "You must count the petals!"

"Oh, is that so?" asked Puss. "I like my way just the same."

"So do I," said the little boy. "All four of us are pretty good chums already."

And the Good Gray Horse whinnied, as much as to say: "I'm a good friend. See what I'm doing—carrying you all so nicely on my big, broad back?"

"That settles it," said Puss. "My Good Gray Horse likes it that way."

"There's our house over there," cried the little girl. "We'd better get off here."

"All right," and Puss helped them down. "Good-by, good-by," and then the two children ran up the path to tell mother all about it.

LITTLE JENNY WREN

AS little Jenny Wren,
Was sitting by her shed
She waggled with her tail,
She nodded with her head.
She waggled with her tail
And nodded with her head,
As little Jennie Wren
Was sitting by her shed.

"May I put up my Good Gray Horse for the night?" asked Puss, Junior.

"You may, my good Sir Cat," replied the little bird. "Hay you will find for his supper, and straw for his bedding."

So Puss, Junior, jumped down and led his steed inside the big red barn and, after tying him in the stall, he looked around for a pitchfork.

"What are you looking for?" asked little Jenny Wren.

"A pitchfork, my dear," announced Puss. "I must spread straw for my horse so that he may rest comfortably, and bring in some hay from the mow for his supper. My paws will not do, so I must ask you where I may find the pitchfork."

"Here it is, my good Sir Cat. Now let me see you use it," answered little Jenny Wren, flying over to the opposite side of the shed and lighting on the handle of a large hay fork.

"Now, my little Lady Wren," cried Puss, after spreading the straw about the stall until he had a fine bed for the horse, "show me, if you please, the haymow, for I must give him some hay."

"I will show you the oats bin, also," said the Wren, "and here is the measure. You must lift this little wooden slide, but see that you don't spill the grain on the floor."

Lifting the slide ever so little, Puss held the measure carefully under the wooden trough until it was filled. Then he carried it over to his horse, who neighed twice, as much as to say, "Thank you."

"And now," said Jenny Wren, "what about yourself, my Lord Cat?"

"Lord Cat!" laughed Puss. "Do lords tend their own steeds? I fear the word Sir is even out of place."

"Never mind," said little Jenny Wren, "you have the manners of a gentleman, and that is enough for me."

"Thank you," said Puss.

"Come, follow me," cried Jenny Wren, and she led Puss into a pretty little cottage close by. "Hang up your cap and place your stick behind the door, and then wash your hands in my room. By that time I shall have supper ready for you."

THE MISCHIEVOUS RAVEN

A FARMER went trotting upon his gray mare—
Bumpety, bumpety, bump!
With his daughter behind him so rosy and fair—
Lumpety, lumpety, lump!

"Can you direct me to the wise man who lives in yonder village?" asked Puss, Junior, bowing politely to the farmer's pretty daughter.

"Whoa!" cried the farmer to his gray mare.

"Isn't he a lovely cat?" whispered his daughter.

"What did you say?" asked the farmer, looking Puss, Junior, over from head to toe.

"I merely inquired," replied Puss, haughtily, "if you could direct me to the wise man in yonder town?"

"Whoa!" cried the farmer as the old gray mare started off. "Whoa, there! Can't you hear the gentleman cat addressing your master?"

"Whoa, Betsy," coaxed the farmer's pretty daughter.

"Well, Sir Cat," said the farmer, as soon as the old mare became quiet, "we have several men in our town who think they are wise, but some of us farmers don't quite agree with them."

And then, all of a sudden, something dreadful happened.

A raven cried croak! And they all tumbled down—

Bumpety, bumpety, bump!

The mare broke her knees, and the farmer his crown—

Lumpety, lumpety, lump!

And, oh, dear me, the farmer's pretty daughter dropped the mirror from her vanity bag, and it broke all to smithereens and she felt so unhappy about it that she began to cry. And then:

The mischievous raven flew laughing away—

Bumpety, bumpety, bump!

And vowed he would serve them the same the next day,

Lumpety, lumpety, lump!

"Botheration!" cried the farmer, rubbing the bump on the top of his head. "That raven is angry because I set up a scarecrow in my cornfield."

"Well, father," said his daughter, "our mare can't take us to town. What shall we do?"

"You get up behind Sir Puss and ride to town," he replied. "I'll take the mare home. That's the best way, I guess."

CANDY TOWN

PUSS, JUNIOR, helped the farmer's pretty daughter into the saddle, and then away went the Good Gray Horse to Candy Town. Well, after maybe a mile and a laugh and smile, Puss said, "I feel just like a Knight of the Round Table, for I have rescued a maiden in distress." And this made the farmer's pretty daughter laugh till her cheeks grew red as two apples.

"Well, then, I shall call you Sir Cat," she said, and this so pleased Puss that he began to purr at a great rate. It was great fun, he thought. And the farmer's daughter thought it great sport, too, I imagine, for she began to sing a little song, and this is the way it went:

"Heigh-ho, over we go,
Pussy and I to town,
What does he wish? A nice little fish,
And I a silken gown.
But where is the money to buy all that,
Unless I may borrow from Sir Pussy Cat?"

"Of course you may," cried Puss. "Just wait till we get to town."

And then the farmer's pretty daughter blushed very red. "I was only in fun," she said.

Puss and the farmer's pretty daughter

"But I wasn't," replied Puss.

"Why, have you enough money?" she asked, giving him a hug.

"Don't squeeze so tight," cried Puss. "We may have an accident, and one is enough for to-day. I hope your father will get the old gray mare home safely."

"Never fear," she replied, "father will attend to that, all right."

"Here we are," said Puss, looking up at a sign-post on which was written, "Candy Town." "Now, where's the shop with the silken gowns?"

"Over there. Don't you see it right next to the baker's shop."

"Oh yes," laughed Puss, "I see it now," and he drew rein in front of the quaint little shop and helped the farmer's daughter to alight.

"Come in with me," she said, "for I'd like to buy what you like." And this so pleased Puss that he made up his mind to buy any gown she fancied, even if it were trimmed with diamonds.

"Do you want that pretty blue one?" he asked, with a smile.

"How did you guess?" she answered. "You are a wonderful cat."

"And now," said Puss, when the gown was wrapped up, "let's have a cream puff in the baker's next door, for I'm sure you're hungry."

"You're a wonderful guesser, Sir Puss," she cried, "indeed you are, as well as a most generous little cat."

THE BRAMBLE BUSH MAN

There was a man in our town,
And he was wondrous wise.
He jumped into a bramble bush
And scratched out both his eyes.
And when he found his eyes were out
He cried with grief and pain,
And jumped into another bush
And scratched them in again.

"That's the man I'm looking for," cried little Puss, Junior. "I wonder where he lives. Maybe he can tell me where to find my father."

"You hold your horse while I ask the baker's wife," said the farmer's pretty daughter.

Pretty soon she came back and said: "He lives in a little house just outside the town. It's not far from our place."

So she and Puss rode away, and she was mighty careful, let me tell you, not to drop the package containing the silk gown which Puss had given her.

Well, by and by they came to the wise man's little house, surrounded by a hedge of bramble bushes; but the wise man himself was nowhere to be seen.

"Let's go around to the barn," said the farmer's pretty daughter. "It's milking time, you know." And, sure enough, there they found him.

"Are you the man who jumped into the bramble bush?" asked Puss.

"Yes, I am. But let me tell you something. They call me a wise man, but I think a man who jumps into a bramble bush is a silly goose."

And then, all of a sudden, the Bramble-bush Man exclaimed: "Goodness me! I once knew a cat who wore red-top boots. A good many years ago there lived near here a miller who had three sons. When he died he left all his property to the two eldest, but to the youngest only a cat. Well, this cat turned out to be a most wonderful cat. Indeed, I heard that he secured a magnificent castle for his young master, as well as the hand of a lovely princess."

"Where does he live?" cried Puss, in great excitement.

"That I cannot tell," replied the Bramble-bush Man, "for I never heard where he went after leaving here."

"Oh, dear me!" sighed little Puss, Junior. "Nobody knows where my father lives." Then he and the farmer's pretty daughter rode away, and in the next story you shall hear what happened at the old farmhouse.

DAFFY-DOWN-DILLY

"DAFFY-DOWN-DILLY has come to town
In a yellow petticoat and a green gown,"

sang the farmer's pretty daughter beneath Puss, Junior's, window. There she stood, bending over her flower bed, the pink strings of her bonnet floating on the morning breeze.

Puss hurriedly pulled on his boots and ran outside. "Good morning! I see your flowers are still in bed."

"Daffy and Down and Dilly are very lazy, I fear," laughed the farmer's pretty daughter; "they'll never get to town to buy a new gown if they don't hurry."

"I hope they won't meet any bad crows on their journey," replied Puss.

"And I hope they won't have any bumpety bumps!" said the farmer's pretty daughter.

Just then the farmer came out of the barn leading Puss, Junior's, Good Gray Horse.

"Good-by," said Puss. "I've had a pleasant visit." And off he rode. By and by, after a while, he met an old crow walking along the top of the fence. He wore a silk hat and carried a cane, but he couldn't lean on it, for the fence rail was so narrow, you see.

"Hello!" said Puss, Junior. And, goodness me! that well-dressed crow nearly lost his balance, he was so startled at Puss, Junior's voice.

Well, as soon as he had caught his breath, he said:

"I have just found a beautiful pearl necklace. Do you think it belongs to the Queen of Hearts?"

Farmer's daughter picking flowers

"I'm sure I don't know," answered Puss. "Suppose you come along with me and maybe we'll find the owner."

So the silk-hatted old crow sat himself down behind Puss, and the Good Gray Horse kicked out his heels, and away they went to the next village, and when they reached there they stopped before the office of the Mother Goose daily newspaper and asked the man who ran the "Lost and Found" advertisements if he knew who had lost a beautiful pearl necklace of twenty-three pearls and a little diamond clasp?

"Let me think," he said, scratching the top of his head, which was as bald as a billiard ball. You see, he was a bald-headed eagle, although I forgot to mention it before.

"You might inquire at a little green house about a mile down the road. A little yellow hen lives there who once had a coral necklace." So Puss said gid-ap to the Good Gray Horse and rode away, and by and by, after a while, they came to the little green house. And when the old crow knocked on the door it was opened by the little yellow hen herself.

"Have you lost a necklace of pearls?" he asked, politely doffing his silk hat.

"Dearie me! Let me look," she answered, hopping back into her little house. Pretty soon she came back with a little jewel case, which was as empty as a Christmas stocking on the Fourth of July.

"Who could have taken it out?" she said.

So the honest old crow handed over the pearl necklace, and went inside for a cup of tea, while Puss said good-by and rode away.

"DONKEY, DONKEY, OLD AND GRAY"

"DONKEY, donkey, old and gray,
Open your mouth and gently bray;
Lift your ears and blow your horn
To wake the world this sleepy morn,"
sang little Puss, Junior.

"I'm no rooster," replied the little donkey. But he gave a gentle bray, just the same, and then the Good Gray Horse neighed, and after that a little adder crawled out of a hole in the ground and said:

"Gracious me! What's all this noise?" And that only goes to show what a dreadful din it must have been, for adders are deaf, so they tell me.

Well, anyhow, Puss didn't wait any longer, but rode away, and by and by, after a while, he met a funny little man with a sack over his back.

"What have you in your bag?" asked Puss, for he felt sorry for the little old man and meant to give him a lift in case he had a heavy load, you see.

"What's that to you?" asked the little old man, with a

scowl. And before you could say "Jack Robinson!" he disappeared inside a stump.

Puss jumped off his Good Gray Horse and peeped in. But he couldn't see anything, only a big black hole. Well, he was just going to turn away when he heard a voice say:

"Mother, I've brought you a bag of gold
For the little pink-and-white pig I sold."

So Puss peeped in again, and pretty soon he saw a tiny light way down deep, like the flicker of a candle. And by and by, as his eyes grew used to the darkness, he saw a

flight of stairs. Then what do you think he did? Jump into the hollow stump and climb down? That's just what he did, and it wasn't long before he found himself in a little hall opposite a small door with a glass knob inside of which was an electric light, which I suppose had been put there by the little old man in case he got home after twelve at night and his wife had blown out the candle.

All of a sudden the door opened and a little old woman, bent and withered, asked, in a shrill voice:

"How dare you come down to our Hollow Stump hall?

I'll cut off your whiskers, tail and all."

"Please, ma'am," said little Puss, Junior, "I won't tell anybody." And I guess he would have climbed up the stairs then and there if he hadn't feared she might cut off his tail when he turned around.

"Let him go, mother," said the little old man. "He would have given me a ride on his horse on my way home had we met sooner." But how he knew that is more than I can tell. "Here, Sir Cat. Take this gold piece and tell neither man nor beast where you got it." And he pushed Puss up the little flight of stairs.

"TICK, TACK, TOO"

ONE day Puss, Junior's, Good Gray Horse lost a shoe.

"Gracious me! I must find a smithy," said Puss, Junior, anxiously. Luckily there was a small village near by, and pretty soon he drew rein in front of a blacksmith shop. But, oh, dear me! there was no one there except a small boy.

Jack Jingle went 'prentice
To make a horseshoe;
He wasted the iron
Till it would not do.
His master came in
And began for to rail.
Said Jack, "The shoe's spoiled,
But 'twill still make a nail."
He tried at the nail,
But, chancing to miss,
Said, "If it won't make a nail,
It shall yet make a hiss."
Then into the water
Threw the hot iron, smack,

"Hiss!" quoth the iron.

"I thought so," said Jack.

"You good for nothing!" cried the blacksmith, coming into the shop, "here's a customer at hand and you have no shoe for his horse."

"How long will it take to make one?" asked Puss, Junior.

"All day and maybe longer," said the smith—"that is, if

you depend on that clumsy lad."

Checking the horse's shoe

"Well, I don't want to depend on him," said Puss, with a grin; "neither do I want to take chances with my good horse."

"Neither shall you, my Lord Cat," replied the smith. "I will see that your horse is well shod, for he is indeed a fine beast."

"He has good legs, has he not?" asked Puss, running his paw down the foreleg of the big gray horse, like a professional horseman.

"He has that," said the blacksmith, "and a fine head, too."

"He's a good roadster," added Puss, seating himself on a three-legged stool while the smith lifted the horse's leg and held it between his knees.

"Yes, he has good feet," said the smith, "and he shall have a fine shoe."

Here a nail, and there a nail, tick, tack, too.

As soon as the shoe was on, Puss, Junior, mounted and rode away. But before he left he turned to Jack and said:

"If at first you don't succeed, try, try again.

Tick, tack, too; learn to make a shoe!

Some day you may turn out ten

If you don't get blue."

LULLABY BABY

MATTHEW, Mark, Luke, and John,
Bless the bed I lie upon.
Four corners to my bed,
Five angels there lie spread;
Two at my head,
Two at my feet,
One at my heart,
My soul to keep.

Puss, Junior, looked in at the window. On a little white bed lay a pretty child.

"Now go to sleep, my little one," softly whispered his mother. "Snuggle down and find a little dream—a little dream about woolly lambs and white daisies."

Then she tiptoed from the room, and no sound was heard except her footsteps on the stairs. Just as she looked through the open door she saw Puss slide down the post that held up the roof of the porch.

"Don't worry, madam," he explained, politely. "I climbed up to see if anyone were at home. Nobody answered the doorbell. But when I saw your little boy I kept very, very still so as not to disturb him."

"You are a good cat," she answered, with a sigh of relief. "I'm glad you were quiet."

"I am very tired, madam," said Puss, "for I have journeyed far to-day. Would it be asking too much if I might sleep on your front porch?"

"You may sleep on a big red cushion in the hall," she replied, "and I will also give you a bowl of milk."

Puss asleep

"May I put my Good Gray Horse in your barn?"

"Of course," she answered. "You will find plenty of hay and oats for his supper."

The Good Gray Horse followed his small master to the stable and was soon made comfortable for the night. Then Puss locked the stable door and brought the key into the house.

"Hang it up on the nail behind the door," said the mother of the little child. "And take off your boots. They make so much noise on the kitchen floor. I fear they will keep my little one awake."

"I will gladly take them off," said Puss, and he placed them behind the door underneath the big barn key.

"My husband will be home very soon," she said, "but if you are very tired I will give you your supper at once."

"I would like it now," said Puss, with a weary sigh. And when he had finished he jumped upon the big red cushion and was soon fast asleep.

THE FIRE

MY Lady Wind, my Lady Wind,
Went round about the house to find
A chink to get her foot in;
She tried the keyhole in the door,
She tried the crevice in the floor,
And drove the chimney soot in.
And then one night when it was dark
She blew up such a tiny spark
That all the house was pothered;
From it she raised up such a flame
As flamed away to Belting Lane,
And White Cross folks were smothered.

Puss, Junior, awoke with a start to find his room filled with smoke. And, oh, dear me! when he opened his door red flames were already crawling up the woodwork.

Running up the stairs two at a time, he pounded on the nursery door and shouted, "Fire! fire!" And then, of course, the baby awoke with a cry.

"Oh, Puss, Junior, what shall I do?" cried the mother, for

the cruel flames were now creeping across the hall.

"Don't open the door," he cried. "The hall is a mass of flames. Climb through the window to the roof of the porch. Be quick!" and he jumped through the little hall window and ran across the roof to the nursery. "Come out here!" he shouted. "Be quick, or the flames will be in your room before you can get out."

Just then, all of a sudden, a ladder was placed against the porch, and a kind fireman with a big red helmet on his head held out his arms. "Give me the baby and follow me." Puss held the top of the ladder to steady it until they were safe on the ground and then slid down without touching the rungs.

"Our pretty house will be burned," sobbed the baby's mother.

"And my red-top boots," cried Puss.

"There goes the stable!" shouted the fireman.

"Goodness me!" cried Puss. "I'd better get my Good Gray Horse!"

By this time the hose was connected and soon the engine was pumping water on the flames. But, oh, dear me! it was too late. The pretty little house quickly burned to the ground—only the big red chimney was left. It was hard work to save the stable, but at last the flames were put out.

"We all must sleep in the hay loft," said Puss.

So the Good Gray Horse was led back into his stall. He was the only one who was comfortable that night, I guess.

THE OLD WOMAN'S RIDDLE

"OH, dear me!" sighed little Puss, Junior, as he thought of his lovely red-top boots which had been destroyed by the fire. "Where shall I get another pair?" for he knew that no ordinary bootmaker had the skill to make boots for a cat. However, when he mounted his Good Gray Horse he found, to his surprise, a couple of gold sovereigns in his pocket. "That's something to be thankful for," he laughed, as he set out upon his journey through Old Mother Goose Land. "I'll stop at the first cobbler shop and see what I can buy."

As he rode gayly along he came across a funny little old woman. On her head was a red sunbonnet and over her shoulders a bright-green shawl. Black-lace mits covered her thin hands, and a pair of white slippers her two little feet.

"My good woman," said Puss, Junior, politely raising his cap as he drew in his Good Gray Horse, "can you tell me where I may find a shoemaker?"

The old woman smiled and said:

"What shoemaker makes shoes without leather,

With all the four elements put together?

Fire and water, earth and air,
And every customer wears a pair."

"I don't know," answered Puss.

"Why, a blacksmith, you goosey!" cried the little old woman, tossing her head.

"I don't want shoes for my Good Gray Horse," said Puss, in a disgusted tone of voice. "I want a pair of shoes for myself."

"Ho, ho!" laughed the little old woman. "So my fine Sir Cat would have a pair of shoes?"

"No, my good woman—a pair of boots!"

"Well, then," she replied, "keep on your way until you reach yonder village. Then cross the bridge and you will soon come to a bootmaker. He will, no doubt, be able to fit a pair of boots to Your Royal Highness's feet." Then she turned up a lane and left Puss to continue his way alone.

"Ah, me!" sighed Puss. "I don't feel a bit like myself without my red-topped boots. Indeed, I feel like an imposter. How will anyone believe that I am Puss in Boots, Junior, if I have no boots?" And, for the first time in his life, he felt discouraged. He had met with many disappointments on his journey through Mother Goose country, but to be without boots seemed almost too hard to bear. Still, with a brave heart, he rode on toward the village. "I have at least the money with which to buy them," he said, "and this is much to be thankful for." Which was a wise saying, I think, for a cat who had been out in the world for so short a time as had little Puss, Junior.

THE COBBLER

"CAN you make me a pair of boots?" asked Puss, Junior, reining in his Good Gray Horse.

The cobbler, who was sitting close to the open window of his little shop, looked up from his bench.

"Will you need two pair?" he asked.

"One pair, my good man," replied Puss, Junior, haughtily. "Do you imagine I wear boots on my front paws?"

"Well, my good Sir Cat," answered the cobbler, "I did not know for certain. I can make two pair as well as one."

"And charge for two pair, I warrant, also," cried Puss, with a grin.

"I can give you fine work," said the cobbler.

"Are you sure?" asked Puss. "My last pair, which was unfortunately burned up in a fire, was made by a royal cobbler."

"I have not made boots for royalty," replied the cobbler, "but I made the shoe in which an old woman lives with so many children that it would take you an hour to count them all. That was some job, let me tell you. One doesn't often live in a shoe, although one may walk in one."

"You don't mean to tell me you made that wonderful shoe?" cried Puss.

"Most certainly, my good Sir Cat."

The Cobbler

"Then you shall make me a pair of boots. And, mind you, my good man, they must have red tops."

"That they shall," said the cobbler. "Dismount, and come into my humble shop. I would measure your feet."

"Perhaps you have a pair on hand that will fit me," said Puss, gazing about the tiny shop.

"I will see," replied the cobbler.

"I am in haste," said Puss, as the cobbler looked over his stock. "I am in haste, for I have yet a long journey before me, and cannot delay. I am in search of my illustrious father, Puss in Boots."

"What!" cried the cobbler. "I once made a pair of boots for a cat. Could it have been the noble Puss in Boots?"

"Tell me where he lives," cried Puss, much excited.

"Ah," replied the cobbler, "that I do not know, for it is many years ago since I made the boots. But here is a pair I think will fit you."

"I would rather that you had told me where my father lives," said little Puss, Junior, "than to have found a pair of boots."

"They are certainly a fine fit," said the cobbler, gazing with admiration at Puss, Junior's, feet.

"Yes," answered Puss, "and here is the money. Good-by," and off rode our little hero, still in search of his father, the famous Puss in Boots.

DOCTOR DRAKE

DOCTOR DRAKE kept a shop,
Of dimensions not large,
In a hole in the haystack
By the side of the yard,
Where he dispensed certain small stones
And one or two gravels,
With sundry rare herbs
He had found in his travels.

"I hope the good doctor's at home," said Puss, as he reined in his Good Gray Horse. "I don't feel at all well today."

So he dismounted and knocked on the front door, and pretty soon the famous duck doctor appeared. He wore a big pair of spectacles and a very high collar, around which was tied a green cravat which matched the feathers of his tail.

"Quack, quack!" said Doctor Drake. "What do you want?"

"I don't know, Doctor," answered Puss, Junior. "I feel far from well; in fact, I think I'm going to be very ill."

"Don't worry," replied Doctor Drake; "that's what we doctors are looking for—sick people. I can cure you, never fear."

"Thank you," said Puss, Junior.

Dr. Drake checking Puss

"Don't thank me yet," answered Doctor Drake; "wait till you're cured—then pay me."

"That will I gladly do," replied Puss, Junior; "only make me feel like myself again."

"I think," said Doctor Drake, after looking at Puss, Junior's, tongue, "you had better give up horseback riding; it's bad for you."

"Oh, dear!" sighed poor Puss, Junior. "What shall I do with my Good Gray Horse?"

"Sell him to me," replied Doctor Drake. "I'm in need of a horse. My practice is growing so large I find it difficult to make my calls."

"Yes, I suppose you do," said Puss. "Your feet are not for walking, but for swimming."

"Right you are," assented the doctor. "Of course, some of my patients live in the pond; but, then, again, a lot of them don't. Take these pills." And the famous duck doctor handed Puss, Junior, a little round box. "One every hour; they'll soon fix you up, all right. Now, how much do you want for your horse?"

Puss, Junior, scratched his head. "What will you give?" he asked, tearfully.

"Twenty-five pounds," replied the doctor.

"Very well," said Puss. "The horse is yours. Give me my money and I will journey along on foot, though it goes hard with me to part with my faithful steed." Then, tucking the box of pills in his pocket, Puss proceeded on his journey.

"NO BIGGER THAN MY THUMB"

HAVING traveled so long on horseback, Puss, Junior, found it hard to resume his journey on foot. However, he manfully set out once more. The pills Doctor Drake had given him made him feel quite frisky, and he ran along at a good rate. In fact, he felt that perhaps he might just as well have kept his Good Gray Horse and taken the chance of becoming really ill. But it was too late now; the bargain had been made and he must make the best of it. So on he jogged, whistling a merry tune to help along his tired feet.

By and by he came to a pretty cottage and, entering the front gate, looked in through the window. At a table sat a woman, singing:

"I had a little husband, no bigger than my thumb;
I put him in a pint pot, and there I bid him drum.
I bought a little horse that galloped up and down;
I saddled him and bridled him and sent him out of town.
I gave him some garters to garter up his hose,
And a little pocket handkerchief to wipe his pretty nose."

"I wish she had given me the little horse," said Puss,

with a sigh, "for I certainly miss my good gray steed."

Just then the woman looked up and, seeing Puss at the window, called out, "Come in, little Sir Cat."

Puss, Junior, jumped nimbly through the open window and stood beside her.

"What do you think of my little husband?"

"He certainly is no bigger than your thumb, madam."

"He is a good little man, all the same," she replied, "and when he's astride of his little horse he makes a fine appearance. Wait, and I will show you how well he can ride."

All of a sudden Puss heard the pawing of hoofs, and there stood the prettiest little horse he had ever seen. It was no larger than a play toy, but well built. A long, silky mane fell over his neck, and a curly tail almost reached to the ground. Then, quick as a wink, the little husband jumped out of the pint pot and vaulted nimbly into the saddle.

"Gid-ap," he cried, and away went the little horse down the road.

"Good-by, madam," cried Puss, running after the tiny horseman. But it was impossible to catch up with him, and pretty soon he disappeared in a cloud of dust. "Well, well," cried Puss to himself, "I had no idea that such a tiny steed could run so fast. Will wonders never cease until I have found my dear father, Puss in Boots?"

Then, taking out his pocket handkerchief, he wiped his forehead. "I shall not despair, however," he said, bravely, "for I have a good pair of legs, and all journeys come to an end at last, so I shall keep merrily on my way."

TELL-TALE-TIT

TELL-TALE-TIT!
Your tongue shall be slit,
And all the dogs in the town
Shall have a little bit.

Oh, dear me! This is what was going to happen to the little girl who had told on her brothers. And all the little dogs were standing around, wagging their tails, as Puss, Junior, passed by.

It was a wonder that the dogs didn't rush out and bark at him, but they were so anxious to get a piece of the little girl's tongue that they didn't notice him at all. Perhaps a cat with boots and spurs, a hat and plume, and a trusty sword didn't look like an ordinary cat to them. And neither was our little traveler.

You see, these little boys had gone into an alley to play marbles, on their way to school, and then the little girl had told her father how they had missed their lessons.

"And Jimmy Jones won all the marbles, and there was a fight! And the teacher kept them in after school!"

"Oh me! oh my!" cried Puss, Junior. "Please don't slit her tongue!"

"But why did you tell tales on your brothers?" asked her father.

"Oh, please don't slit her tongue!" cried Puss, Junior, again.

"That's what they did in Mother Goose."

"It must have been very long ago in the dark ages," answered Puss, laying hold of his sword.

"Well, it's only a rhyme!" laughed her father, picking up his little girl and hugging her. "Come on, Sir Cat, follow me. You are quite a Knight of the Round Table. If a fair lady be in distress you are her champion!"

Pretty soon all three came to a little house and Puss was invited to come in and play. There was a nice swing under an old apple tree, and soon he was swinging as high as the little girl could push him. All of a sudden he jumped out up among the branches and hung on to a limb, just like a trapeze performer.

"I once was with a circus," he explained, sliding down the rope and turning a somersault on the ground.

Just then the little boys came in the gate and how they did laugh! And Jimmy gave Puss all the marbles which he had won, and his father, who had been sitting on the porch watching the fun, gave Puss a dollar. After that they all went in for lunch and Puss didn't start out on his journey until late in the afternoon.

ON THE WAY

"ON the way, on the way,
To see my father, old and gray.
Faster still, my good gray steed,
Over hill and flowering mead.
"Faster, faster, Good Gray Horse,
Hasten swiftly on your course,
Till I see the stately towers
Where my father spends his hours."

"Urge me not too much!" panted the faithful steed. "I'm doing my best, but these hills have made me short of breath."

Dear me! I forgot to tell you that the Good Gray Horse had run away from the famous Doctor Drake and had caught up to Puss, Junior, just as I commenced this story.

"Forgive me," cried little Puss, Junior. "In my anxiety to see my father I have been selfish." And he slipped a lump of sugar into the mouth of the Good Gray Horse.

Well, after several miles had gone by, Puss drew rein at a drinking trough beside the road, where his faithful steed drank long and deep. And as they rested a while, who should fly by but a busy bumblebee, buzzing from flower to flower.

He was a jolly-looking bee, and presently he said to Puss, "Whither are you bound, my good Sir Cat?"

Riding to the castle

"To the castle of my Lord of Carabas," replied our little traveler. "I'm seeking my father, who is seneschal to my lord."

"Ah, is that so?" exclaimed the bee. "These are stirring times. I heard only last week that my Lord of Carabas was

going to war!"

"What!" exclaimed our small hero, jumping to his feet and clapping his paw to his sword. "I must hurry on!"

"Bravely spoken," answered the bee. "I have seen many soldiers at the castle of late. Indeed, the country is all excitement—flags flying, drums beating, men drilling, women scraping lint. All is bustle and hustle."

"And what brings you so far from there?" inquired Puss, replacing his sword in his scabbard.

"My two good wings," replied the bumblebee, and he laughed as he dove head first into a flower after its dewy sweetness.

"Come, little master," cried the Good Gray Horse. "I am rested. Let us hasten on our journey."

Puss bade good-by to the golden bumblebee and sprang once more into the saddle. And the Good Gray Horse threw out his heels and galloped off toward the castle of my Lord of Carabas, but evening came upon them and they were still far from their destination, so Puss dismounted for the night beneath a grove of trees.

LITTLE BOY BLUE

YOU remember in the last story that Puss and his Good Gray Horse had camped in a grove of trees for the night. Well, just as Puss was about to curl up and take a little trip to dreamland he heard a voice singing:

"Little Boy Blue,
Come, leave your toys.
It's time to wash hands
For little boys.
"Supper is ready,
You must not wait.
Tuck in your napkin
And don't tip your plate.
"Oh, where is Boy Blue?
Let's all take a peep.
He's there on the sofa,
Fast asleep."

Puss opened his eyes and saw a little light twinkling through the trees. So he got up and went toward it to find that it shone from the window of a small cottage. As he knocked on the door he thought, "I may be asked to spend the night, and that will be much more comfortable than lying beneath the trees." And it turned out just as he thought. The pretty woman who opened the door asked him in, saying, softly:

"Tiptoe in, my dear Puss, Junior, for Boy Blue has just gone to sleep." And you know how softly a cat can tiptoe! But of course he first slipped off his red-topped boots with their clanking spurs.

Then Boy Blue's mother gave Puss, Junior, some milk and cake, and after that he put his Good Gray Horse in the stable and came back to sit down by the fire.

Over the mantelpiece hung a silver horn, and as Puss looked up at it he remembered long ago in Old Mother Goose Land a little Boy Blue who blew his horn to call the cows from the fields of corn.

"Does your little Boy Blue go to sleep in a haystack?"

"No, my dear," laughingly replied his mother, "but his father did. And that's the horn he used to blow in the early morn to call the cows and the woolly sheep when under the haystack he'd fallen asleep."

"I met him once, a long time ago," said little Puss, Junior. "I remember the place quite well. He carried me on his shoulder over to see little Miss Muffet who sat on a tuffet, and she gave us some curds and whey till a horrid old spider sat down beside us and frightened her away."

"And so you were the little cat who was with him, were you?" said little Boy Blue's mother.

But Puss didn't answer, for he had fallen fast asleep and was dreaming that he was once more with his dear father, the famous Puss in Boots.

ALPHABET TOWN

NOW let me see. Where did I leave off in the last story? Oh yes, I remember now. Little Puss, Junior, had fallen asleep in the house where little Boy Blue lived. Yes, Puss had fallen asleep in front of the fireplace over which hung the silver horn that called the cows from the fields of corn. Well, the next morning the horn began blowing all by itself, and this, of course, woke up everybody in the house; so Puss washed his face and hands and curled his whiskers and after that he pulled on his red-topped boots and was ready for breakfast. Then Mrs. Boy Blue came downstairs with little Boy Blue. He was only three years old, but he could blow a horn, though I don't think the cows paid much attention to him, for they knew he was only doing it in fun, you see.

Well, after breakfast, Puss, Junior, bade them all good-by and mounted his Good Gray Horse, and by and by, after he had ridden many a mile, he came to a very queer place—it was called Alphabet Town. But the strangest thing of all was that the alphabet was alive. Yes, from A to Z it was alive, and Puss was so interested that he drew rein at the gates of Alphabet Town because, he said to himself, "If I expect to get through Mother Goose Land I must learn the alphabet, and the sooner I learn it the sooner I shall see my dear father." So he went up to the schoolhouse and this is what he learned:

A was an Ant who worked all the day.
B was a Butterfly, flitting away.
C was a Cherry that hung on a tree.
D was a Daisy that grew on the lea.
E was an Elm that stood by the school.
F was a Frog that lived in a pool
G was a Goat with a beard on his face.
H was a Horse that won a fine race.
I was an Insect that fed on a peach.
J was a Jay Bird whose song was a screech.
K was a Kitten that played with a string.
L was a Lambkin that browsed in the spring.
M was a Magpie that stole a gold spoon.
N was the Nest where she slept 'neath the moon.
O was the Oak Tree that held safe the nest.
P was a Pigeon with soft purple vest.
Q was a Quail that was shot with a gun.
R was a Rooster that woke up the sun.
S was a Snail that was awfully slow.
T was a Turtle, no faster, you know.
U was a Unicorn; of him you have heard.
V was a Vulture, a rapacious bird.
W was a Wren that made a sweet noise.
X was a Xmas Tree, covered with toys.
Y was a Yule Log, dragged through the snow.
Z was a Zero when winter winds blow.

And I think when I tell you that Puss learned this alphabet in less than half an hour you will agree with me he was a very bright cat.

LUCY LOCKET

"GID-AP!" said Puss, Junior. "Gid-ap, my good steed, for we must hasten on. 'Tis yet a long ways we must journey ere I find my illustrious father, Puss in Boots."

The Good Gray Horse quickened his pace, and soon many a mile was left behind.

At length Puss saw a little girl in the doorway of a cottage.

Lucy Locket
Lost her pocket;
Kitty Fisher
Found it;
Nothing in it,
Nothing in it,
But the binding
Round it.

"Whoa!" cried Puss. "Can I help you, miss?"

"I'm so disappointed!" cried the little girl. "I thought there might be a bright penny inside."

"Are you sure there isn't?" asked Puss, sympathetically. "Do you want a penny very much?"

"Yes," replied the child.

"Well, here's one," replied Puss, thrusting his paw into his pocket and bringing out a bright penny. Leaning down from his horse, he handed it to the little maid.

"What are you going to buy with it?" he asked.

"Peppermint stick," she answered. "Peppermint stick with red rings all around it."

Puss and the Little Maid

"That sounds pretty nice," said Puss. "Where's the candy shop?"

"Just over there," she replied, pointing to a small shop on the opposite side of the street.

"Let's go in," suggested Puss, dismounting and tying his Good Gray Horse to the hitching post.

The candy shop smelled very nice. Molasses candy in long yellow coils lay in the glass cases. Sticks of pink-and-white peppermint candy stood in big glass bowls with shiny glass stoppers. Chocolate drops were ranged in long glass dishes. There were gumdrops and marshmallows, and goodness knows what all. Puss thrust his paw deep into his pocket, for he knew that one little penny wouldn't go very far in this candy shop.

"What other kind do you like?" he asked.

"Why don't you call me Kitty?" laughed the little maid. "My name is Kitty Fisher."

Just then another little girl appeared.

"Hello, Lucy Locket!" cried Kitty.

"I've just lost my pocket," said Lucy. "Did you happen to find it?"

"Yes," replied Kitty, "but there was nothing in it. Just a ribbon round it."

"That's 'cause I took out my penny," answered Lucy,

"and I'm going to spend it right here before I lose it."

Soon both little girls had eaten their peppermint-candy sticks. And after Puss had given his Good Gray Horse a big lump of sugar he mounted and rode away.

TOM, THE PIPER'S SON

"TOM was a piper's son,
He learned to play when he was young;
But all the tune that he could play
Was 'Over the hills and far away.'"

"Well, it's a pretty fine tune," said Puss, Junior, to himself, as the strains from Tom's pipe came clear and sweet across the meadow. "I wish I could play as well." Again the music came down the breeze, clear and sweet, and pretty soon Tom came capering toward him, followed by a crowd of boys and girls.

"Heigh-ho!" laughed Puss. "Here they come, dancing away, as if they had nothing to do but play all the day long."

"Over the hills and far away!" piped Tom.

"Good morning!" cried Puss.

"Come and dance," said the piper's son, taking the pipe from his mouth; "come and have a merry dance. Make those red-topped booties prance."

"Then play a merry jig," answered Puss, catching up a small pig and waltzing him around at a giddy rate.

"Hold on!" cried the pig. "I'm getting dizzy."

"I won't let you fall," replied Puss, with a grin.

"Let go!" squeaked the pig. "I tell you I'm getting dizzy!"

"Well, why didn't you say 'let go' at first," laughed Puss. "You said, 'hold on.'"

By this time the poor pig was so out of breath that he rolled over on his side and lay quite still until a small boy said:

"Your tail is all twisted from dancing around and around."

"Nonsense!" replied the pig, sitting up. "Pigs' tails are always twisted. Dancing makes your head go around, but it doesn't curl your tail."

Then all of a sudden Tom commenced to play again.

"Oh, please don't!" cried the breathless pig. "I don't want to dance any more."

Tom with his pipe did play with such skill

That those who heard him could never stand still;

Whenever they heard him they began to dance—

Even pigs on their hind legs would after him prance.

And, goodness me! it was such wonderful music that even Puss couldn't keep still, but must needs dance with a little girl in a blue dress until Tom was out of breath and too tired to play any longer.

OLD DAME TROT

AS soon as Tom, the piper's son, stopped playing everybody sat down to rest, even the little pig who had been waltzing about on his hind legs. He didn't try to run away. I guess he was too tired for that. Pretty soon he took out a yellow handkerchief and wiped the perspiration from his pink nose, and after that the little girl in blue asked Puss, Junior, where he had learned to dance.

"At Mademoiselle Feline's dancing school," replied Puss. "She taught twenty-one little kittens twice a week."

Just then, all of a sudden, Tom, the piper's son, jumped to his feet and started off, and before very long

He met Old Dame Trot with a basket of eggs;
He used his pipe and she used her legs;
She danced about till the eggs were all broke;
She began to fret, but he laughed at the joke.

"I think it very mean of you to break an old lady's eggs," cried Puss.

"I'm sorry your eggs are broken," cried Tom to Old Dame Trot. "If you'll come with me I'll show you where there's a nest full of eggs; it's in the dry grass under the raspberry bushes in yonder meadow."

But the old lady had gone only a few steps when
Tom saw a cross fellow beating an ass
Heavy laden with pots, pans, dishes, and glass;
He took out his pipe and played them a tune,
And the jackass's load was lightened full soon.

"It serves that fellow right," cried Puss. "His donkey had too heavy a load."

And while the tin pans were flying about and clattering on the stones the old lady climbed over the fence.

"There goes the hen to her nest now!" shouted the children.

"I'll play her a tune and while she's dancing you pick up the eggs and give them to Old Dame Trot," cried Tom.

Of course as soon as the music commenced the little hen began to dance. And when all the eggs were in the old lady's basket he stopped playing, but the little hen was so provoked that she went straight home to the barnyard.

BOBBY SHAFTO

AS Puss, Junior, rode along on his Good Gray Horse he passed a pretty cottage near the roadway. And the roses that climbed over the front porch were so fragrant and the voice of the girl floating through the open window was so sweet that he stopped to listen.

"Bobby Shafto roams the skies
With silver goggles on his eyes.
A lonely girl am I who sighs
For pretty Bobby Shafto.

"Bobby Shafto's bright and fair,
Very gay and debonair;
He's the king of all the air,
Bonny Bobby Shafto.

"His airship is the fastest one
That races with the golden sun,
And when his azure voyage is done,
Pretty Bobby Shafto.

"He's promised he will marry me,
And then how happy I shall be;

We two shall sail the starry sea,

I and Bobby Shafto!"

Singer sharing cream

Pretty soon the owner of the lovely voice looked out of the window and when she saw Puss she asked him to come in and sit on the front porch while she went for some cream. So Puss tied his Good Gray Horse to the hitching post and, opening the little gate, sat down on the doorsteps. After he had finished drinking the cream she asked him to tell her where he was going with his lovely red-topped boots and long feather plume. And would he take out his sword and show it to her? All this made him very proud, and of course

he thought she was a lovely little girl.

Well, after a while they spied an airship in the sky. Pretty soon it came nearer and nearer till finally it landed in a field close by. The little girl and Puss jumped up and ran as fast as they could across the road and through the fence.

Throwing her arms around Bobby Shafto, she cried, "He's the king of all the air."

Then he took off his silver goggles and shook hands with Puss, and soon they all came back to the little cottage and had ice cream and sponge cake, and Bobby Shafto fed the Good Gray Horse a quart of oats, and after that Puss said good-by and rode away.

LITTLE ROBIN REDBREAST

"WELL, well!" said Puss to himself as he left Bobby Shafto and the little girl. "To think I should see an airship in Mother Goose country!"

By and by he heard a little bird singing:

"Little Robin Redbreast sat upon a tree,

Up went pussy cat, and down went he;

Down came pussy cat, away robin ran;

Said Little Robin Redbreast, 'Catch me if you can!'

Little Robin Redbreast jumped upon a wall,

Pussy cat jumped after him, and almost got a fall;

Little Robin chirped and sang, and what did pussy say?

Pussy cat said, 'Mew,' and Robin flew away."

"What are you trying to do?" asked Puss, Junior, stopping under the tree and looking up at the pussy cat.

"I'm not trying to do anything," replied the pussy cat, crossly. "I was wishing I had wings."

"They'd be very convenient at times," said Puss, with a grin.

"Indeed they would," answered the pussy cat. "I'd rather have them than red-topped boots."

"Perhaps," answered Puss. "But I have found my boots most helpful. Do you know," he continued, "if people would be a little more contented with what they have I think they'd get more."

Cat climbing a tree

The pussy cat looked ashamed of herself. "What you say is very true. I suppose I ought to be thankful that I have such strong claws. It's not hard work climbing trees, and as for running, my legs carry me very well. Perhaps I don't need wings, after all."

"Well, I never saw a flying cat," admitted Puss, Junior, "although I've seen some remarkable things since I started out to find my father, Puss in Boots."

"So you are a traveler," said the pussy cat, jumping down from the wall and walking up to Puss. "How long have you been looking for your father?"

"A long, long time," replied Puss, Junior. "Do you know, sometimes I almost get discouraged, for this is a big world and at times I feel so very, very small."

"Well, you come home with me," said the pussy cat. "You need a good rest. I think you're tired out."

THE ELF CHILD

LITTLE Miss Pussy Cat had a house
That was very trim and neat.
But, oh, dear me! there wasn't a mouse
For little Miss Pussy to eat.

"There's a nice, soft cushion on the window seat," she said to Puss, Junior. "Why don't you take a nap?"

And as he was very tired with his long journey, he curled up and was soon fast asleep. But, oh, dear me! all of a sudden there came a loud knocking on the door, and when Miss Pussy opened it there stood a little dog with a very loud bark. And then, of course, Puss woke up with a start.

"Please make him go away," said Miss Pussy Cat. "I'm dreadfully afraid of dogs."

So Puss picked up his big stick and the little dog ran away as fast as he could, never again to bother little Miss Pussy Cat. And shall I tell you why? It was because when he finally stopped running he found himself in the woods where the fairies lived.

And when they saw him they said to one another, "This little dog has been up to mischief, for if not, why should he run so fast?" And then the king of the fairies said, "I will see that he makes no further mischief," and he waved his silver wand, and the little dog turned into a dogwood flower that blooms every year in the same spot under the great shady trees.

Of course little Miss Pussy wondered for a long time why she never saw him, until, one day, Jennie Wren, who lived in the woods, told her what the fairies had done.

Well, pretty soon Puss, Junior, set out once more to find his father, and as he went along he whistled a tune to keep up his spirits, when, all of a sudden, he heard a little low whistle. And there in the road, a few feet ahead, was a tiny little man dressed in green with a high-peaked hat on his head.

"I've never heard a whistling cat,

So come to the wood with me,

And whistle a tune to my elfin child

Under the greenwood tree."

Then little Puss, Junior, followed the queer little dwarf and by and by, after a while, they came to a glen in the wood where, under a great oak tree, sat the prettiest little elf you ever saw. He was playing with a gray squirrel and a striped chipmunk, but when he saw Puss he gave a glad shout and away went the squirrel and the chipmunk. But he didn't care, for a cat with boots was something he had never seen.

"Teach him to whistle, Sir Cat," said the dwarf.

So Puss sat down by the elf child and by and by, just as the stars began to twinkle from the sky, he had taught him to whistle. And, would you believe it? it sounded like a bird, it was so sweet and clear. And after that Puss went on his way to find his father, happy to think that he had proved so good a music master.

And some day, in another book, I will tell you how little Puss, Junior, finds his dear father.